animal attack!

TIGER ATTACKS

Suzanne J. Murdico

HIGH interest books

Children's Press
A Division of Grolier Publishing
New York / London / Hong Kong / Sydney
Danbury, Connecticut

For my husband, Vinnie

Photo Credits: p. 4 © Tom Brakefield/Corbis; p. 7 Tom McHugh © California Academy of Sciences; p. 8 © William Dow/Corbis; p. 11, 16 © Terry Whittaker/ Frank Lane Picture Agency/Corbis; pp. 13, 19, 37 © Digital Stock; p. 15 © Keren Su/Corbis; p. 20 © Digital Vision; p. 22 © Kennan Ward/Corbis; p. 23 © Richard A. Cooke/Corbis; p. 25 by Kim Sonsky; p. 28 © Gary Vestal/ IndexStock; p. 31 © Philip Perry/Frank Lane Picture Agency/Corbis; p. 33 © Farrell Grehan/Corbis; p. 34 © Hulton-Deutsch Collection/Corbis.

Visit Children's Press on the Internet at:
http://publishing.grolier.com

Library of Congress Cataloging-in-Publication Data

Murdico, Suzanne J.
   Tiger Attacks / by Suzanne Murdico.
      p. cm.—(Animal attack!)
   Includes bibliographical references (p. 43) and index.
   Summary: Examines the history of tiger attacks on humans, discussing loss
      of habitat, long-term captivity, the endangered status of tigers, and plans
      for their protection.
   ISBN 0-516-23319-x (lib. bdg.) —ISBN 0-516-23519-2 (pbk.)
      1. Tigers—Behavior—Juvenile literature. 2. Animal attacks—Juvenile litera-
      ture. [1.
   Tigers.] I. Title.

QL737.C23 M87 2000
599.756'156 21—dc21
                                                        99-040448

contents

For hundreds of years, tigers and humans lived around each other peacefully. Tigers usually attacked humans only when angered or when a female tiger was protecting her cubs. However, in the past thirty years peace between tigers and humans has disappeared. Humans have built homes in what was once the tigers' habitat. The habitat is land where the tigers live.

Tigers are the largest of the world's big cats. Almost all members of the animal kingdom fear tigers. An adult male tiger can be 10 feet long (2.8m) and weigh more than 500 pounds (225kg). An adult female is about 9 feet long (2.7m) and weighs about 300 pounds (135kg).

In recent years, tigers have begun to attack humans more often. Part of the reason is that

This Sumatran tiger is an endangered species because so few of them still live in the wild.

there are fewer kinds of animals around that tigers eat (called prey). As humans use up the tiger habitat, they also use the land where tigers hunt for food. Some hungry tigers have now become man-eaters. They hunt humans as prey.

Until the early 1900s, there were almost 100,000 tigers in Asia. Asia is one of the seven continents. At one time, there were eight different breeds (types) of tigers. Different types of tigers are called subspecies. Three of those subspecies are no longer alive. They are extinct. These are the Caspian tiger, the Javan tiger, and the Balinese tiger. The last five living subspecies are hard to find in the wild. These are the Bengal, Siberian, South Chinese, Sumatran, and Indo-Chinese tigers. Tigers are an endangered species. This means their population in the wild is very low. They may become extinct without special protection by the government. Only five to seven thousand tigers still exist in the wild. Tigers generally live for about fifteen years in the wild.

This saber-toothed tiger is extinct. It is an ancestor of today's tigers.

chapter one

WHEN PEOPLE GET TOO CLOSE

Mahat Awang lives in a village on a rubber plantation in eastern Malaysia. One Saturday, he went to check a trap that he had set to catch wild boars. From out of the bushes, a tiger suddenly jumped on Mahat. The tiger began biting Mahat's head and clawing his body. Mahat struggled with the tiger and tried to reach for his hunting knife. But he couldn't reach his knife.

"I tried to fight back but got bitten on my hands and the back of my head," Mahat told the newspaper, the New Straits Times. *"After attacking me, the tiger ran into the bushes and disappeared."*

Tigers can run fast.

Mahat survived the attack. He needed fifty stitches on his hands and head to repair the damage done by the tiger. No one is sure why the tiger gave up the fight. Mahat Awang is glad that it did!

WHY TIGERS ATTACK

Tigers generally attack something or someone for one of three reasons: to get food, to defend or find new land, or to protect their young.

Food

Tigers eat meat. Meat-eaters are called carnivores. Most tigers eat a variety of medium- or large-sized wild animals. These include deer, elk, antelope, and wild boar. Tigers hunt alone and at night. Animals that hunt at night are called nocturnal. A tiger may travel between 10 and 20 miles (16–32km) each night. Tigers use their sharp senses of sight, hearing, and smell to find prey.

When a tiger sees its prey, it hides in the tall grasses. The tiger's striped fur helps it hide. When

Tigers tear at the hides of animals to get at the meat. Tigers usually hunt at night.

a tiger hunts its prey, it moves slowly. A tiger's careful movements keep the prey from seeing where the tiger is. Once the tiger gets close, it

did you know?

A tiger's stripes aren't only on its fur. Beneath its fur, a tiger's skin is also striped in the exact pattern as the fur stripes!

lowers its body into a crouch.

Then the tiger jumps quickly from the bushes and grabs its prey. The tiger uses its front claws and heavy body to knock the prey to the ground. The tiger uses its powerful jaws and pointed teeth to bite the animal's throat and break its neck.

The tiger drags the dead animal to the bushes. There it eats its prey for hours or even days. A tiger may eat more than 50 pounds (22.5kg) of meat in a single night! Tigers must hunt often because they don't always catch what they hunt.

The tiger's body is built for hunting and killing large animals. To make jumping easier, their back legs are longer than their front legs. Also, the front legs and shoulders have large muscles. Their front

Tigers have sharp teeth and powerful jaws.

When People Get Too Close

paws have long, sharp claws. Tigers use their claws to attack and eat prey, and to defend themselves against other tigers. These claws can be pulled back into the paws. Also, a tiger's jaws have lots of muscles that help it to crush its prey.

Territory

The increase in tiger attacks on humans has been blamed on the loss of the tigers' habitat and on illegal hunting. Illegal hunting is called poaching. In their natural habitat, male tigers live alone. They need about 24 square miles (62 square kilometers) of their own. There they live, hunt, and mate. For almost forty years, huge areas of Asian forests and jungles have been cleared to make way for human use. These areas are places where tigers once lived. They have been replaced by coffee plantations, farms, factories, and houses. The loss of this land forces tigers to look for new places to live and hunt.

Another problem is that hunters illegally kill

A Siberian tiger is eating a chicken

deer and wild boar. These animals are the tigers' prey. When hungry tigers can't find prey in the jungle, they go to nearby towns. There they find goats, chickens, and cattle to kill and eat. Sometimes they even find people.

"People are beginning to understand that we do not have control over wild animals. We are invading their space," Laurie Macdonald explained to

Tiger cubs need their mother's milk and her protection from other wild animals.

Sierra Magazine. Ms. Macdonald is the head of the Sierra Club's National Wildlife Committee. Meetings between tigers and humans "are a risk we take when we enter these animals' territories. We have to accept the [outcome] of our actions."

PROTECTION

Female tigers are very protective of their cubs. Female tigers are called tigresses. Their cubs are born blind and helpless. Tigresses will attack humans, male tigers, or other predators who want to harm their cubs. Tiger cubs are rarely seen in the jungle because the mothers carefully hide their young. Female tigers will share prey with their cubs and feed the cubs first. If there is not enough food, a tigress will go hungry so that her cubs may eat.

chapter two

THE MAN-EATERS

Khammual Thongtam is a forest ranger at a wildlife conservation park near Bangkok, Thailand. Ranger Thongtam lives in the staff quarters at the park. One day, Khammual was washing clothes on his balcony when a tiger appeared. The tiger caught him off guard. Khammal had no gun and nowhere to escape. The huge animal jumped 3 feet (91cm) from the ground to the balcony and attacked the man.

The tiger bit and clawed the ranger's arms. Another ranger heard Khammual's screams and came to help. The tiger then attacked the second ranger. It began biting and clawing him, too. The

A tiger can leap high in the air.

two men screamed and people came running to help them. The tiger got scared and jumped down from the balcony and ran into the forest. Both

rangers survived the attack but were seriously injured.

During the night, the hungry tiger came back. Another ranger then shot and killed the animal.

"Tigers usually just run away when they smell humans, except when they are hurt or starving," Khammual told the Associated Press.

After the tiger was killed, a bullet from an old wound was found in its right front leg. Rangers explained that this injury probably kept the tiger from hunting its usual prey. The animal's hunger caused it to search other places for food. Without guns, humans are defenseless against a hungry tiger. This is because humans move more slowly than most wild animals.

HUMANS AS PREY

Although tigers are carnivorous, most do not eat humans. This has changed in recent years. The number of man-eaters has risen in several parts of Asia.

A tiger's stripes are as unique as a human's fingerprints.

MAN-EATERS IN INDONESIA

In 1999, Sumatran tigers killed and ate at least nine people in a week in Lampung. Lampung is an area in southern Indonesia. Most of these people were attacked as they worked in the coffee fields or as they collected firewood.

In Indonesia, Sumatran tigers are protected by law. It is illegal to hunt and kill them. However, over the years, much of the tigers' natural habitat has been lost because the land has been turned into plantations or destroyed by illegal logging. Experts say that there are not many Sumatran tigers left living in the jungles. Many of these tigers have also been killed by hunters. These poachers sell tiger organs (such as the heart, liver, and kidneys) and bones. Some people believe that the body parts can be used to help cure certain diseases.

A Sumatran tiger

When a tiger gets a taste for human flesh, hunters must be sent to kill the animal.

MAN-EATERS IN MALAYSIA

Just as in Indonesia, man-eating tigers have appeared in Malaysia. In 1998, man-eating tigers killed two people and attacked at least two others. Since only twelve attacks had taken place in the twenty years before, this increase has worried the government. In Malaysia, tigers are a protected species. There are only about five hundred to six hundred tigers that live in the wild. Several organizations that help to protect endangered animals are concerned about the Malaysian tigers. The World Wildlife Fund (WWF) is one of these organizations. The WWF is concerned that the tiger populations will continue to decrease. They want governments to protect the tigers' habitat.

MAN-EATERS IN RUSSIA

In Russia, attacks by man-eating tigers have also become more common. In a one-month period, two men were killed by tigers. One man was a hunter whose head was bitten by a female tiger. He crawled 40 feet (12m) in the snow before bleeding to death. The other man was attacked by a tiger and half-eaten as he walked to the train station. Russia now has a group of people—called the Tiger Group—to track down and kill man-eating tigers.

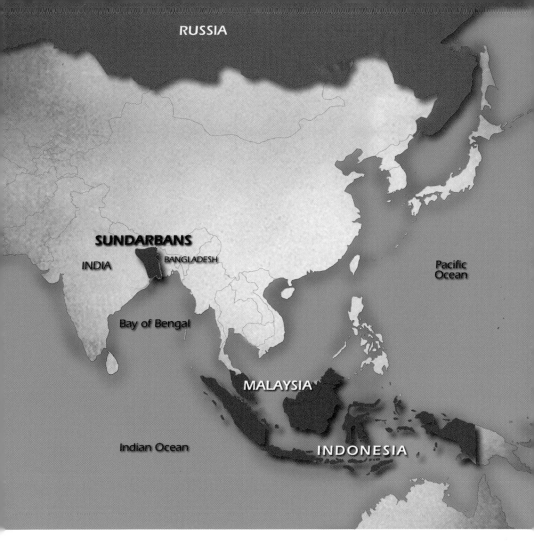

MAN-EATERS OF
THE SUNDARBANS

The largest population of man-eating tigers are found in the Sundarbans. The Sundarbans is a huge forest area between India and Bangladesh.

People in the Sundarbans have tried different tricks to keep tigers from attacking humans. One trick is for forest workers to wear face masks on the backs of their heads. Because tigers attack from behind, a person who seems to have a face on both sides of the head is less likely to be attacked. Another trick to keep tigers from attacking is to set out clay figures that look like humans. These figures are wired with electricity. If a tiger attacks one of these clay figures, the animal gets an electric shock. The people hope that the tiger will learn to stay away from humans.

Almost five hundred tigers live in this area. There are many man-eating tigers there. No people live in the Sundarbans, but it is a popular place for fishing, gathering firewood, and collecting honey.

For the past twenty-five years, more than eight hundred people have been killed and eaten by these tigers. Stories told about the man-eaters of the Sundarbans have become well-known around the world. Villagers claim that these tigers can float in the water and climb onto the deck of a fisherman's boat without making a sound. Suddenly there's a splash in the water, and the fisherman has vanished! The idea that cats don't like water does not apply to tigers. Tigers love the water and are excellent swimmers.

The reason tigers in the Sundarbans have killed so many people remains a mystery. Some people believe that it has to do with the lack of fresh water in the Sundarbans. Others think that the muddy swampland of the area makes it difficult for tigers to catch their usual prey. However, no one really knows for sure why the Sundarbans is home to so many man-eating tigers.

chapter three

TIGERS IN CAPTIVITY

Jaunell Waldo is a forty-five-year-old California woman. She received a special birthday gift from a friend. The gift was a photo session with Kuma. Kuma is a 340-pound (153kg) Bengal tiger at Marine World, a wild animal park in California. Waldo posed for the photograph by kneeling down on a raised platform as Kuma lay next to her. One of Kuma's trainers held the tiger's leash. For some reason, the tiger stood up. Ms. Waldo stood up too, but she stumbled and fell off the platform.

Kuma became frightened by this sudden move, and the tiger leaped on top of the woman. The animal then clamped his enormous jaws around her.

Tigers have very good eyesight and sharp hearing.

He bit her head and neck. The bites were deep. The tiger's sharp teeth put holes in Ms. Waldo's skull and neck. During the attack, Kuma's trainer was still holding the tiger's leash. He had been pulled off the platform when Kuma leaped on Ms. Waldo. As the woman began screaming, the trainer yanked on the leash and pulled Kuma's head away from her.

Then another trainer jumped in to help. Kuma scratched the man's back with his sharp claws. Both of Kuma's trainers screamed commands at the animal. One of them hit Kuma on the head with a cane to try to distract the tiger. Kuma soon calmed down. The attack was over in a matter of seconds. Jaunell Waldo was flown to a nearby hospital, where she had surgery for her injuries.

Kuma had taken part in about 100 photo sessions with park visitors. So why did the two-year-old tiger attack that time? Jeff Jouett, a Marine World spokesman, explained that Kuma was very frightened. "It was unusual for him to be pulled

Circus trainers have nowhere to run if tigers decide to attack.

and beaten. With all the screaming going on, he reacted instinctively in an aggressive manner," Jouett told the newspaper, the *San Jose Chronicle*.

Kuma is like many other "tame" tigers in theme parks and circuses. He had been raised by trainers from the time he was just a few weeks old. Most trained tigers are used to hearing unusual noises and seeing people move around them. Usually, they won't become scared when something out of the ordinary happens. Even so, attacks such as Kuma's do happen.

"Basically, you are dealing with a wild animal," explains David Robinett of the San Francisco Zoo. "Regardless of how much you work with it and train it, there is always the potential for danger."

Some experts think that tigers raised in captivity will not kill because they are not taught to kill. Mr. Robinett disagrees. "There is always a certain amount of killer instinct there," he says.

TIGERS IN CIRCUSES

Tigers in other types of captivity, such as a circus, have also been known to attack. These attacks usually occur against the animal's trainer or keeper. In some circuses, tigers and other large animals are kept in cages. Like other wild animals, tigers are used to living in the large, open areas of forests and jungles. Being kept in a cage disturbs animals. If disturbed, tigers will become angry and may attack people who come near them.

Circus tigers may attack as a result of being kept in small cages.

This tiger may attack his trainers at any time.

In 1998, outside London, England, a tiger bit off and swallowed a worker's arm. This attack happened at the Chipperfield Circus. The worker had put his arm in the tiger's cage to feed the animal. Only one month earlier, a Bengal tiger had attacked a member of the Chipperfield family. During a photo session, the tiger locked onto Richard Chipperfield's head with its jaws. The man's brother, Graham, also an animal trainer, had to shoot the tiger.

The National Anti-Vivisection Society accused the circus of maltreating and beating the animals. This organization is a British animal rights group that also claimed the Chipperfield Circus kept its lions and tigers in small cages for more than 90 percent of the time. Such captivity may have caused these animals to attack.

TIGERS IN ZOOS

Most large zoos no longer keep animals in cages. However, some small or private zoos still do. Even in small zoos, tiger attacks don't happen often. When attacks do occur, it's usually when a zookeeper hasn't followed the rules about how to be near the animals.

Such an attack occurred at the Fort Wayne Children's Zoo, in Fort Wayne, Indiana. Besar is the zoo's only tiger. Besar attacked a zookeeper as she was cleaning the animal's cage. The keeper did not follow zoo rules. Besar was in the cage while the keeper was working. According to zoo rules, the tiger should have been in a different pen while the keeper was in the cage.

"These aren't pets," explains Jim Anderson, director of the zoo. "The animal was dangerous before today and will be after today."

THE FUTURE OF THE BIG CATS

There are two major problems that must be overcome to save tigers from extinction. One is illegal hunting, called poaching. The other is loss of tiger habitat.

Poaching

Poaching has been a problem since hunting wild animals was outlawed decades ago. However, the illegal selling of animal hides, trophy heads, and body parts happens all over the world. Some people will pay huge amounts of money for tiger hides which are used as rugs.

As you learned earlier, many Asians buy tiger

Protecting tigers in the wild is the goal of many wildlife organizations.

parts to eat. Some Asian people want to buy the bones, liver, kidneys, and other organs of tigers. These buyers use such parts as medicines. Yet there is no medical proof that eating these organs helps the human body in any way. Today, there are programs used to teach people that it's wrong to believe such myths. Such myths must be defeated before human greed defeats the tigers.

Loss of Habitat

Large areas of natural tiger habitat disappear every day around the world. However, there is hope for the big cats' survival. To save tiger habitats from growing human communities, many countries worldwide have set aside land for endangered wildlife to live in peace and freedom. Large amounts of public land have been set aside for use only by endangered wildlife.

Such a place exists in western India. It is called Tadoba National Park. Another is Khao Yai National Park in Thailand. There is also Negara National Park in western Malaysia. All of these parks have set aside land as wildlife preserves. These lands will help save tigers and other endangered animals. These parks offer animals space to roam, hunt prey, and mate. It is hoped that attacks by tigers on humans will no longer be a problem in such places. With the help of the Russian government, the U.S. government, and the World Wildlife Fund, another tiger preserve project is under way in the Russian Far East. These two governments and many other organizations are trying to help save the Siberian tiger. With such help, maybe the beautiful big cats can live in the wild as they once did.

FACT SHEET

Subspecies and Geographic Locations

Bengal (Indian) Tiger: India,
   Nepal, Bangladesh, Bhutan
Indo-Chinese Tiger: Thailand,
   Vietnam, Malaysia, Laos,
   Cambodia, Myanmar
Siberian Tiger: eastern Russia,
   China, and North Korea
South Chinese Tiger: southern
   and central China
Sumatran Tiger: island of
   Sumatra in Indonesia
Caspian Tiger: extinct
Balinese Tiger: extinct
Javan Tiger: extinct

Life Span

Fifteen years in the wild
Sixteen to eighteen years in zoos

The tiger heads on the map show
where tigers are found in east
and southeast Asia.

new words

captivity the state of being confined

carnivore an animal that eats meat

coexist to exist at the same time

conservation the careful protection of animals

endangered threatened with extinction

extinct no longer in existence

habitat an area where an animal naturally lives and grows

nocturnal being active at night

poaching illegal hunting of animals

predator an animal that hunts and kills other animals

prey an animal that is killed and eaten for food

sanctuary a place where animals are protected from hunters

stalk to hunt

territory an area that is occupied and defended by an animal or a group of animals

for further reading

Bailey, Jill. *Save the Tiger*. Madison, NJ: Steck-Vaughn Library, 1990.

DuTemple, Lesley A. *Tigers*. Minneapolis: Lerner Publications Company, 1996.

Harman, Amanda. *Tigers*. Tarrytown, NY: Benchmark Books, 1996.

Levine, Stuart P. *The Tiger*. San Diego, CA: Lucent Books, Inc., 1999.

Perry, Phyllis J. *The Snow Cats*. Danbury, CT: Franklin Watts, 1997.

Scidensticker, John. *Tigers*. Stillwater, MN: Voyager Press, 1996.

World Wildlife Fund-United States
1250 24th Street, NW
Washington, DC 20037-1175
(202) 293-4800
e-mail: wwfus@worldwildlife.org
Web site: *www.worldwildlife.org*

Endangered Wildlife Trust
346 Smith Ridge Road
New Canaan, CT 06840
(203) 966-2748
Web site: *www.ewt.org*

Tiger Missing Link Foundation
17544 FM 14
Tyler, TX 75706
(903) 858-1008
Web site: *www.tigerlink.com*

Web Sites

Animal Attack Files

http://www.igorilla.com/gorilla/animal/

This site offers a great selection of news articles describing recent attacks on humans by animals. Included is a link to book lists for further reading.

World Wildlife Fund

http://worldwildlife.org/

Here you will find educational information on endangered lands, endangered animals, and global threats to the environment. There is a great photo gallery included at this site. Also, learn about conservation in your community.

Endangered Wildlife Trust

http://www.ewt.org.za/

Learn about the research, awareness, and conservation projects that the trust supports. You can

read up-to-date news articles about endangered animals and look through their photo gallery.

Tiger Watch
http://hometown.aol.com/tigertrail/index.htm
This site offers research facts about the biology of tigers, tiger facts, and conservation efforts. Also included is a gallery of tiger photos.

index

ABOUT THE AUTHOR

Suzanne J. Murdico is a freelance writer who specializes in educational books. She has a degree in English and is the author of ten nonfiction books for children and teens. Suzanne has always loved animals. She did her college internship in the public relations department at the Philadelphia Zoo. Suzanne lives in New Jersey with her husband and their two tabby cats.